AMERICAN SYMBOLS
SÍMBOLOS DE AMÉRICA

THE **NATIONAL ANTHEM**

El **HIMNO NACIONAL**

Joe Gaspar
Traducción al español: Eduardo Alamán

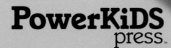

PowerKiDS
press.
New York

Published in 2014 by The Rosen Publishing Group, Inc.
29 East 21st Street, New York, NY 10010

First Edition

Editor: Amelie von Zumbusch
Book Design: Colleen Bialecki

Traducción al español: Eduardo Alamán

Photo Credits: Cover Elyse Lewin/Photographer's Choice/Getty Images; p. 5 Charlotte Nation/Stone+/Getty Images; p. 7 Dilip Vishwanat/Getty Images Sport/Getty Images; p. 9 Jemal Countess/WireImage/Getty Images; p. 11 Paul J. Richards/AFP/Getty Images; p. 13 Brendan Smialowski/AFP/Getty Images; p. 15 Eric Broder Van Dyke/Shutterstock.com; p. 17 © iStockphoto.com/laflor; p. 19 Hulton Archive/Getty Images; p. 21 Image Source/Getty Images; p. 23 iStockphoto/Thinkstock.

Library of Congress Cataloging-in-Publication Data

Gaspar, Joe.
The National Anthem = El Himno Nacional / by Joe Gaspar; traduccion al espanol, Eduardo Alaman.
  p. cm. — (American symbols = simbolos de America)
Parallel title: El Himno Nacional.
In English and Spanish.
Includes index.
ISBN 978-1-4777-1208-5 (library binding)
1. Star-spangled banner (Song)—Juvenile literature. 2. United States—History—War of 1812—Flags—Juvenile literature. 3. Flags—United States—History—19th century—Juvenile literature. 4. Key, Francis Scott,—1779–1843—Juvenile literature. I. Gaspar, Joe. II. Alaman, Eduardo. III. Title.
ML3561.S8 G37 2014
782.42—dc23

Websites: Due to the changing nature of Internet links, PowerKids Press has developed an online list of websites related to the subject of this book. This site is updated regularly. Please use this link to access the list: www.powerkidslinks.com/pkras/anthem/

Manufactured in the United States of America

CPSIA Compliance Information: Batch #S13PK4: For Further Information contact Rosen Publishing, New York, New York at 1-800-237-9932

CONTENTS

CONTENIDO

Can you **sing** "The Star-Spangled Banner?"

Puedes **cantar** The Star-Spangled Banner (La bandera llena de estrellas)?

4

It is our national anthem.

Es el himno de nuestro país.

It has been since 1931.

Lo ha sido desde 1931.

It is fun to sing.

_____

Es divertido cantarlo.

It has four verses.

Tiene cuatro versos.

You hear it at **games**.

Lo escuchas durante
los **partidos**.

The music is by John Stafford Smith.

La música fue escrita por John Stafford Smith.

The words are by Francis Scott Key.

La letra del himno fue escrita por Francis Scott Key.

He wrote them in 1814.

_____

Key lo escribió en 1814.

They are about a **flag**.

El himno habla de
la **bandera**.

WORDS TO KNOW/
PALABRAS QUE DEBES SABER

flag
(la) bandera

game
(el) partido

sing
cantar

INDEX

ÍNDICE